Truth, Justice and the Companionship of Owls

Peter Riley

Longbarrow Press

Published in 2019 by
Longbarrow Press
76 Holme Lane
Sheffield
S6 4JW

www.longbarrowpress.com

Printed by T.J. International Ltd,
Padstow, Cornwall

ISBN 978-1-906175-38-2

First edition

Contents

Pennine Tales

i.

Red flicker through the trees. The last minibus
leaves from the station heading for the tops,
full of ancestors from Halifax: farmers, publicans,
clerks, ghosts, with my name in their notebooks,
wanting me back in the peace and jubilee
of diurnal normality. But they have caught
the wrong bus and will be delivered into nothing,
the nothing of death, where they came from,
to welcome me home. Passing the abandoned chapel
they start singing hymns, and will soon begin to fade.
Down here another train rolls in and the dark river
splashes past on the stones of demolished mills, let go of me.

ii.

For that peace I would halt the wind in the trees
whose watery rustlings enclose us at night
like the books on the bookshelves, leaning
this way and that like old men in bus queues
after the pubs have closed and a red light flickers
in the station forecourt meaning it's on its way
and will drop you all one by one at the ends
of long farm tracks. You'll reach your doors in
darkness and wind leaving various lost strangers
standing on moorland roads with nowhere to go
and sinking into a forgotten past through miles
of gorse and heather over towards Haworth.

iii.

The last train for Leeds leaves, gathering speed
on the embankment. It won't now stop
at Luddendenfoot where Branwell Brontë
attempted briefly to inhabit the 19th Century.
Brontë shadows in the signal box, unreachable
save by word, for word brings me nearer, moon
behind ridge-top cloud, word brings us together
in mutual need, my sisters. I turned my back
and headed south for richer spaces as full
in their ways of grandfathers and mills and local ale.
The words for peace and hope fetch me here
where all you are because of something we know.

iv.

It is grand to walk round the block
in a warm evening, the river alongside
chattering, love is a gravitation, follow
me to the last post. The lights are on
in several canal boats, the water there
perfectly still. Full moon with aura
over the crest, night bands of cirrus
across the sky or a passed jet. One
or two owls. Not a soul to be seen
on the dark towpath but up
at the station pub they are singing
the hymn of last or lasting hope.

v.

Accused of seeking beauty in the face
of human wrong, "complicit" and so we do,
and cast it against human harm, utter calm
in the face of the lie itself, knowing what
we have always known. The world
could not be more open than it is,
the diamonds of the heart jostle and fizz
and spread sparks into the fields of consolation
where our hurts do the hora. Let us join them.
Let us fail with some footlift, some persiflage
behind a glowing window onto the cold canal
where the future is quite carefully formed.

vi.

Words are not magic crystals. What's that
faint tapping in the night? It is Ted Hughes,
wishing he'd stayed in Mytholmroyd and not
been made into a hero by hungry clerks
or his wife into a martyr by ideologues. Tap.
Tap. Is that you? Can you hear me? In the night,
in the dark, are we safe for the moment? Do you
remember a brief time in Cambridge meadows
safe from print police and prizes? And the Penguins
waddle past above our icy graves bearing
their own biographies across the frozen flats:
an egg-dance and a swift fish.

vii.

Owls call in the wooded hillside, is anything safe
from devaluation? They do not plead for themselves
or even for the species. The night is their instrument
and the graves in the subsoil their amplifiers.
Mournful calling falling sound between
rural and urban, between spattered sky
and turning ground my mind turns round,
an idea of justice drawing daily closer to its
impossible centre. Call again, let us know that
a wholeness and nothing else no other turn or tune
keeps the cart on the road the song in the air
and all heaven's politicians under lock and key.

viii.

Another wind like tonight's and tomorrow
the leaves will all have flown. Perhaps
I am not so far from the poetical centre
perhaps it is around me, calling my name
and passing by like a ship in the night, wearing
its eminence as a floral garland stripped by terrestrial
wind to a metal crown, worn by the night guard.
Blast your music on us, passing transport, turbulence
on the platform when the express rushes through
and we shall sing the song of delayed passengers
which goes: We will get there yet we will
wait for ever and cancel the debt.

ix.

Out of the Hare & Hounds 11:20 pm with Mike Haslam
and stand on the edge of the moors. Difficult
to believe that a small bus will come and
pick us up. There is nothing here but stone walls
and distance. We are alone. We are nowhere.
We are in the length and breadth of a dark nowhere
which encompasses the world. In this vast nowhere
the refugees at Calais cover their heads in dark tents
the township people murmur under iron roofs
contented for the moment, worried for the future
and along the road a lighted vehicle appears
in Old Town where old trusts survive and seek us.

x.

Shine into tomorrow like the bus headlights
on the high road between fields and moor,
stone walls curving by the land. Michael
gets off at the cancelled pub and we swoop down
leaving him to walk home on the dark road.
Bits of fence and house-front left and right telling us
where we are, which is increasingly not a nowhere.
Returning to our rest we remain in transmission,
we are in contact, we burn in the night
top to bottom of the landscape and pass on
the favours and curses of the visiting night spirits.
Small electric lights burn in the canal-side cabins.

xi.

Wilful impoverishment, O evening star,
how will you guide us past that? How
do we meet hands over the hilltops when
both of us are vapour? Your work is to hold
the sky together, mine to hand in a letter of
complaint at the Town Hall, but your reach is
greater, covering the dome from east to west
and thus sang the old man: O Night, O Book,
O star in the water... Listen, there's a man
in the streets of Leeds in the rain in the big
Christmas crowds singing into a microphone
"take my whole life too."

xii.

Jeremy Prynne I wish I could play the archlute
to your physical ear. And we would walk together
over the dark moorlands believing in something
I don't know what. Some call, some night music of
stop and start, some tremble between beliefs.
I walk with Wordsworth, and poor Clare,
Shakespeare who repeatedly disappears,
and Hardy, guide and spokesman. Sometimes
hundreds of us walk the tired dark page, water
with stars in it leaking into our boots, eradicating belief.
But a crowd worth joining. Not a protest.
A recognition of earth in the moon's clearance.

xiii.

The final disclosure of the world, to end on an open fifth
like a forest path in the Vienna Woods ending in a prospect
of small towns distributed across the agricultural plain
seeming to say that all is well enough as far as we know
or everything worth knowing about is under permanent threat.
Sometimes at night alone on the open moors conditions
of time past surround and tramp about me, deaths
of people I knew when young, auntie this uncle that
a few broken memories but still that face smiling up
at me and fading into the dark ground they never knew
with a wish for a child's success. At the end of this walk maybe
a pub and a bed, a plum and a pat on the head for the wolf child.

xiv.

Ending at an open space, the whole dome of sky
bonded over us and the star of the sea
washed up on an earthen bank. The question
about poverty and exploitation shining in the darkness.
Will anyone ever answer? Each year I walk slower
on stubborn ground and hear more. The voices
on the night moor are stones in a wall, rained on
until the water reaches the footing and
flees to the town. Until society and economy
are brought to support each other, until the trees
fall into the river, until the stones weep,
there are badly swollen people among us.

xv.

Thousands of lights spread over valley and hill,
windows, street lamps, earth forms netted in lights.
And in the dark corridors between these lights
do the dead still go from door to door begging
for sustenance? Tell us it has not been all in vain.
And do the living-room lights then twinkle, are they
Co-operative lights? Or does a choir sing in the
dark distance, under the fabric of the town,
"We never thought it would come to this."
It will come to more yet and take my cold hand.
The world tips slightly, the clock croaks Amen,
that we should see such clarity again.

xvi.

Thousands of house rows and blocks of flats
spread over valley and hill, Blackburn, Accrington,
the Preston line across north of Manchester,
the living rooms displayed when it gets dark
and the train rides the embankment. Why so
powerless? Later a few farm lights on the black hill
and all this was once a field of action, a place
that mattered, by acts of combination where
free thought walks in the sky by day and night.
To arrive, to stay, to become old, to learn
the details, the stone paths strung over the hills,
the football record, when the next train is due.

xvii.

Spinal fluids rush to the edge of my right shoulder-blade
and stand there in rank, planning trouble. Is this
another ancestral cohort from Halifax trying to
dispirit me with milky tea in vestries?
Return, lad, back down the family steps, learn
that geriatric shuffle your father was so good at …
But I shall sing Schubertian trance-music to them
and they'll break rank and wander over to the pub.
And when it rains in the night all the little black biddies
and bugs that live under the stones start singing
in pips and squeaks, psalms of lamentation
and gratitude, and a ballad of the future.

xviii.

Come all you little vermin that dwell under stones
crushed underfoot of the earth and make together
a faint hissing and rustling in the night which
grows greater towards the central principle
and the separate sounds build to a chorus
saying that 500 years of degradation and humiliation
is as nothing to us, we can persist ten times as long
working towards a modern condition which
recognises at long last the day of the many.
For the capital aristocracy are still in charge
and there is no end to our patience and assurance.
Take your partners for the last waltz.

xix.

I shall lay me down on this bank of sweet primroses
with violets intermixed, and wait
for the world to settle into itself at last,
into its own house, dreaming of waking
to the sound of sparrows at the window,
dreaming the persistence of labour
under the feet of the new masters
and at night the owls will keep vigil
as our heads sink deeper into pillows,
turning as the earth turns, tilting
into the mountain crest at dawn, where
our numbers are called in finally.

xx.

There is a History in all men's lives
and some are arrayed like goldfinches
that fly away and are not seen. Soldier,
friend, who says that language is
either normal or poetical? what is this
I'm saying with but a feathery brightness
hoping to become a stony rightness? At night the black
water falling through the lock is heavy with stars
and I think of my connections, my soldiers,
as points of light in a vast dark loss. A history
that someone could use, like a stone house in the
hills available to friends and family.

xxi.

Fresh and gentle hilltop wind blowing damp
as I stand outside the Hare & Hounds waiting for a bus
by a stone wall. Me and the thistle and the willowherb.
Streamlet falls into culvert. This is where the place
shows its meaning as an accumulating guarantee
that there will always be a freshness, in whispered words
of justice and audible reassurance of human standing,
standing outside a pub, standing beside a moor,
where all the answers are shared. Allow my voice
some ear, world masters, I stand nowhere counting
the generations of workers and thinkers
as the bright chariot approaches.

xxii.

Night goods train fills the valley with its noise
spread out over all the houses and gone. People
check their watches: 10:50. The music draws
our thoughts into the distance and re-affirms
presence at home, site of mind/heart decisions,
for the home line is the world line and everyone
knowing this goes to bed after 10:50 pulling blankets
to the chin. Everyone the same as everyone else
(Lassie, lie near me) and then we are free
to speak, out and for. Canada geese and
mallards on the canal, sparrows and tits
in the small trees, owls in the night hollows.

xxiii.

We get back from Crete and a bus goes past,
from Halifax. I am stretched and bundled
in these distances but when do I get to see
the Goddess descending? On the swings perhaps
of the municipal park on the wings perhaps
of song on Ted's face as he jumps from a Bridestone
to the mossy ground, what fairer chance is there?
Then the wind blows and the trees shed
their leaves which fall across the sky
curled red yellow and brown and settle
on the surface of the canal. The Goddess
of any death smiles, weeps, fades.

xxiv.

Upper Colden. Snow swirls at the doors
of stone farmhouses, thistle vibrating in the wind,
snow cloud approaching up the valley.
This is true north. Later the moon rises and people
behind rows of small windows take tablets,
set the clock, do what they usually do.

In sleep, in dream song,
the daylight ghosts are laid
and trouble us no more.
In silence nightlong
a life's debts are paid
at the open door.

Hushings

i.

Coming out of Widdop Gate at night, a black hill
across the valley with lights of farms here and there,
all of stone. Lights like stars, stars like sores and welts
on a dark body, stars and stripes on a black man's back.
And there's me, placing a first foot on the stone
steps of Banks Lane Council School, 1945,
a first step into the nation, to be followed
by 68 years starred and scarred with gains and losses
and gates opening upward and pits closing down.
The land lies dark in the night's width,
seeing to itself, all the black slopes
nursing fledglings for all they're worth.

ii.

Then I stood stock still before a motet
by Antoine Brumel in which I seemed to hear
encompassed in angels' wings and stone arches
a working woman singing to get her child to sleep,
like a solitary reaper singing, "My wounds
are not yours. I have come to know the heartland
as work, control of breath, a totally dependent
child in my arms like a scythe." Hush, little sword,
you are my word in the world and together
we'll walk through fear and cold weather
constructing in tended thought our own reward
as slowly first light on the hill admits widening regard.

iii.

Yes, I thought, passing under Nutclough Mill at night,
I want to live under these lights. Passing under
the rain, the persistence, the flowers that bloom in
the spring *(tra-la)*, walking under the failure.
Something happened which tipped half the globe:
common language and interchangeable currency
and the swans singing goodbye on the reservoir.
What remains, small children being carried home,
the dark street under those steady lights,
the closed shops, the flowers folded for the night
and always water running over stone.
Yes, to live here, extant, come what might.

iv.

Two buzzards wheeling over the top of the woods
and one of them says to the other, What
do you see down there, brother, with your
little eye? I see a lot of language stumbling
on fissured paths through the woods,
seeking a footing, straddling an omission.
I see the earth turning about my sight-line,
pubs and workplaces, black beetles on a
communications mast, the honesty box.
In the high fields, in the pastures, there's a man
sitting on a rock singing Solveig's Song.
The sheep stand around listening.

v.

The turning circle at Crimsworth. The 595
waits there, running its engine to keep warm.
Not a house in sight. Stripped, wind-swept
moorland, gritstone walls in bad repair, snow
quite likely. Here we wait, as if waiting
for the return of truthful politics. And in
all this land, this nothing-much, there are
hidden values, seeds waiting to announce themselves
as cotton grass and bugle. Then the time
falls due, and we set off again, down
into the bowl, down onto the palm
of a cupped hand. The band plays "Set You Free".

vi.

The wooded valley at night. Nobody speaks.
Nobody believes. Nobody knows what's happening.
The river runs swiftly, water running off the moors
where the heather has been burnt, for the apes
of eminence must go shooting again.
Nobody knows what they say to each other
or what they plan for the world. Some movement
passes through the trees. The plants and beasts
of the valley sides are perfectly clear, they seek
their operational limits in open competition.
Up on the tops the black grouse crouch under
dead heather in the dark, knowing nothing.

vii.

Crimsworth turning circle. The 594 sits there with its lights on.
The driver's not to be seen. It is my turn now
to be silent, to lean against a bus in the middle
of the night not saying where the meeting is,
at which our hopes will collide or coincide.
A slow and solemn trust draws me onwards;
it is night itself, the secret solution, wrapped
around the heart, the dark simplicity of mutuality.
And who's this five-year-old mounting for the
first time the stone steps that lead up to the
assembly hall, there to be taught to sing.
All Things Bright and Beautiful.

viii.

Politics crying out for a moral imperative,
and it's not poetry's job. Poetry can wait
like an old minibus in a garage while
we sleep, slightly losing oil. The family ghosts
get into the house at night and creep around
trying not to make noises because
a frightened population is a dangerous one.
At this point the poem goes to sleep, and dreams
of vocal consonance, of the cooing pigeon
and the purring cat, the mooing milk-machine
and the stirring of the vast vat where hope's tide
gathers and advances to the horizon.

ix.

Little shoes stamping the road, trying
to keep up with the procession, admission
to a world which cures all other worlds.
At the gate of the Sunday school he joins the queue.
The crow examines his passport, the hedgehog his account,
the fox explains the delay, the seal croons his tune
and he shakes hands with the thrush. Many years later
he lies alone again, in a dark bedroom with window
onto a lit street with no traffic, and a busy brain
calculates his progress to this far distant point.
The animal shadows round his bed seem to have forgiven
all the desires entrusted to the rusting of the years.

x.

Standing by the great mill wheel turning
I seem to hear the earth busy balancing
its accounts from the river to the edge of the sky
and all the voices make one mutual cry,
a harmony stretched across the road
with an archway in it towards the distant woods.
At Swinside the cold grey boulders stand shoulder
to shoulder in a perfect ringing, around a perfectly
flat disc or turning circle, where routes meet and cross
and the hand is taken and the song is sung, sunk
in peaceful trust. Well, let us hope so. The big wheel
frightens me, I am busy with dustpan behind the door.

xi.

You tourists who come and go, pause and note
that this place is blocked and split by failed
hopes galore, and full of pawned god-
heads gone for lunch to our great joy.
Ay, enjoy a long, long lunch you keystones
of all the collapsed mills and closed libraries.
Civic controllers, to follow you I lose my way
among your wars and a sweet laugh recalls
hope galore, not because it is small.
Ostinato, obstinately I take the stony road
and again the thrush welcomes me
and again the end calls and falls, take good note.

xii.

The greater thoughts break themselves against despair
but a twiddle and a trill bring them all back home.
Mr Wilson's Second Liners do "Set You Free" in Hebden
Bridge centre. The renewal is sealed in the song, and
the dead return to this life here, to this rain and
this company and the language running alongside. The in-
explicably absent son opens his arms, and every single soul
returns to all the places it has ever known. Mr Wilson's
band enacts the joyous return from the cemetery
spreading mortality over the land and the living stand
like rows of megaliths in tidal grass, suspended in greater
thought, for hope stands firm in the common tongue.

xiii.

Returning from the Stanley Spencer exhibition at Wakefield
having to wait for an hour in Mirfield it becomes obvious:
you find some place to live and you move in.
Once the door is closed the voice gains in strength
and proposes a self, a focus that cruises out across
the shop fronts and chapels, the appeals for volunteers
to run the library, the clinic, the police station, the town
hall, the whole vast empty and hungry State, the state
we are in. The shrivelling. Whisper to me good ghost,
I'm here, my shoes decked in sparkling dirt, waiting
for messages in an abandoned village. Whisper me
the terms of endearment, and government in equity.

xiv.

Sunlight filtered through thin cloud at mid-day
touches the stone outside the Hare & Hounds.
The stone beams back its own shades, not
illuminated but responding, accepting the offer.
Such a spectre orders the regional ghosts
back to the tumuli and abandoned warehouses
where they belong. Such a spectre sets
history back in our own hands, the stilled mills
come to life, the great engines hiss and thrust,
plumes of smoke rising across the valley. And this
spectre in the throat, this hope in the hand, that won't,
that just will not, abandon the children.

xv.

These spectres are no more than thoughts
but they are international. So I go to
the International Restaurant in Bradford
and think my way through a mixed thali
that all the hills and rivers are of course
the vocabulary of our lamentation. So go no
further than the foot of the hill, the stream pouring
over the stone and think to the heights, O waly, waly,
love is hard, as we know, and dearly bought.
And O the rain, and O the snow, but the truth
is held firm, shown to me in Bradford
as a necklace of mind trances on the chitraveena.

xvi.

Up here at Old Chamber looking over the whole valley
from the door of the Honesty Hut, which is never locked,
the guiding star invisible in the sky (signalling goodbye) while
everything gained for centuries is chucked away without
a second thought and for what? For the end of the chorus,
the end of public truth. So we sing together all the
songs of the centuries one by one and nobody hears us.
Up here above the town the site is so fair, the weather
so kind and the sense of our silent singing is passed from
generation to generation. And who's that over there,
half a mile away, waiting for a bus outside the Hare
& Hounds? And here it comes.

xvii.

A bright afternoon at the hushings, a far
prospect from the ruins of commerce, far over
the fawn-backed moors and the long hills
to a distant reservoir, Colne to the left, squatting
on the landscape like an iced cake – Who would guess?
that the ruins might open and 100 tons of water
descend on us and the state crack apart and ever
after the heartless govern the streets. Who would
suppose the end of the hours, the end of one and
every true love, the last kind thought in the land.
Blood on the primrose petal, mucus on the stone,
definitions of justice engraved on the bone.

xviii.

That gentle harmonic murmur in The Trades Club
as they join in "Only Remembered" or "Shallow Brown",
a firm, and quiet, moan for the world's departure.
In the night outside the interconnected power centres
abscond, leaving us alone to work out by ourselves
that death is a beautiful ending to any song, the path to it
full of stones like the paths on the moors. New families,
viols and lutes, some sweet day, when the war is over, we'll
walk together over the top and delicately down the stone steps,
down the stone, down the air, down the darkness
singing *Dove sei, amato bene?* viewing bright below
everything we have. And I said to the star, Eat me.

Ring Cairns

i.

Don't tell me to report anything suspicious that I may see.
Tell me instead how with rosy steps the morn advancing
drives the shades of night away

and standing barefoot on a Herdwick rug,
earthfast, I'll call to the common mind
that it is needed, urgently, its common care.

And I'll call out again to the fleeting senses
until they pause, and turn back
to claim their seats in the parliament of minds.

The message, about morning, the way it is sung,
as simple as can be, a homely sentence
and a country step towards a future worth having.

Like holding a young child on a wall to see the sea
for the first time, at dawn, the world's thought-task,
vast, and simple, and irreversible.

ii.

The bit of pavement in Birstall where
Jo Cox was killed, near the library. I take
a photograph, of nothing, to remind me

of nothing, and how her name sails clear of it
how her speech is written on a history and
the killer's name forgotten soon as said.

All we demanded was justness, to see it
brightening the air over as plain a piece of pavement
as you'll find between love and hell.

And still a report echoes across the dull town
and still an answer stands in the language.
The photo goes into war records under "Whatever".

iii.

The cairn circle on the edge of Midgley Moor,
swamped in heather – can just about make out
a raised curve of ground, and just about an answer.

In this figure lies the circle of our sorrows,
why we form a band. A buried failure touches
the edge of the mind with its lost wishes and

measured tread. This watch must never be deserted,
this discount never claimed, this tenure fixed in sorrow
maintained among night's pearly drapings.

A circle dance, like the one in Sardinia, turning
its backs on the latest invasion, opening and closing gates
to a trance music, and gently bobbing up and down.

Counting the time, which is the answer, the succession.
So we reckon we can just about keep our senses clear
through public contradiction, and set off down

the causied track, so fair and honoured a route
to the Hare & Hounds, and there's Mr Haslam
in his dark hat, bobbing up and down.

iv.

Footnote. Here I stepped into a hole in the moor.
It is full of them. They are it. A ring cairn is made
to set rightful minds at peace by burying them

under heaps of stones within a circular bank. That's
us, our failures, handing the world over to monsters,
take this and let us die, we say, we have had enough.

And our failures lie crouched there, set to watch
in all directions by the turning ring and to ask
all our old questions for ever. When will plain truth

be decisive? Has it all been in vain? What time is it?
Mr Haslam was bobbing up and down because
he had just read an account in which every faintest

hope is blasted and every foot is in a hole and the best, the
cleverest, turns deceiver. The Landlord settles Michael,
sunshine with rain, and that thing is still there up there.

v.

Handel, offered "What God ordains, is right"
to end the final chorus of Act II of *Jephtha*
crossed it out and wrote, "Whatever is, is right"

(Pope) and stamped it bitterly into the faces
of London Tories in a series of halts culminating
in a shout, and another shout, and a final shout. *Is right.*

Ist recht. It is remembered in our little ring dances,
our tumuli and our small crafts, never free
of the bitter touch, nor the moon's sad relapse.

Tonight the Hill Millies dance at Birchcliffe
and you know perfectly well, Mr Interlocutor,
that most of what is is not right and is not good either.

The children lost at sea, the families broken
by war and paranoia, it all beams at us in the quick
glitter of an ankle-bell, and the concluding shout.

vi.

We get back from Malta and a cyclist goes past
heading for Todmorden, where some of the lost songs
are still known. He pedals fast, he might be the last

archivist with any chance of addressing the turn of fate
face to face, *inde ira et lacrimae* while over the hills the
long grey hills the airs play freely and late in the day

the bats emerge from the eaves of our houses.
To secure the earth, to record the sun's stations
through thin gaps between limestone slabs marked with

slow vine tracery, at dawn, my bonnie boy.
That's one way but go anyway, find the lover
in a low cottage who has dared to speak. Repeat

what she speaks. Late at night the three quarter moon
through slats reminds us to notate while we can
between anger and tears the last waltz, the song left over.

vii.

Our long history on small scraps of paper.
Your voice, trailing over the night airs.
Your words, standing at corners of the solution

saying, Go from my window, go. For the world
sends too much to our houses, demanding
that we sing it, there are bills to be paid.

But under the song is the speaking voice
saying what must be said, that only the strength
of international law will save us from falling

completely away and the blue-nosed cowboy rides
the pink-bummed baboon to eternity
if someone doesn't call the lie. The night is cold.

The wind and the rain will bring you back again
and the door will not be locked. Love is bold
and the night is long, and our history is what was said.

viii.

There's a notice in the post office window saying
Death Mornings. Tuesdays 10:30. All welcome. Coffee.
And up on the wide moors a New Orleans funeral band

is processing in a circle, shouting at each revolution,
You are incredible. Then they disappear and
it is a *makam* trio lamenting in quarter tones

the fall of Constantinople, a foot in a hole, the end
of truthful politics as of effective international law.
From now we are back in unprotected servitude.

As water falls through air to earth, as fathers seek
their lost children across deserts and seas in city-
states and sad ports, as the whole of congress is

a history of nothing until the spectres behind our minds
fight for the right to speak true and they weep
in the streets to see violence offered to young children

because they are "not Us". In which case nor am I,
or any of us, party to any Us there is. We'll gather
in small rooms on Tuesdays for madrigals and gin.

ix.

Many's the night's rest you've robbed me of,
but you never will do it again. Who are you?
Come with me. We'll hold our coats close

and walk to the Methodist graveyard half
way up the hill to Heptonstall and all
the town's lights will be on the ground. We'll hear

the town speaking in its own languages,
screams and roars, ambulances and motorbikes,
and the shout when they collide.

Listen, the creature squirming in those lights
is telling you something, a history of love
and war. Attend closely to this dance. Look down,

look down low, for nothing will ever come from above
but bombs and empty lights, that remember nothing
and settle like moths on our eyelids, and die there.

x.

We are incredible. Our tombs say so. We are
the children of work-destroyed bodies. We walk up
to the circular cemetery at midnight

and shout: *Lazare, veni foras!* I know you're in there!
Come out of it. And tell us the truth,
after the event, do we wake up or what?

And if we do, what does the world matter? No,
he dances, and the owls signal along the woods each
to each in heraldic hoots: Brother, sister, it turns out

there is no knowing, as we've always known.
They say no more but, credible creatures, defy
the regression of polity, crunch a few mice and amen.

xi.

I remember the chorus of wolves from London Zoo
late at night over Primrose Hill as we lay there
glad of each other, the mind for the time settled,

settled into the time, which was about midnight
and the window open. In love there is no certainty
to be had but a trust and the wolves howled

over our heads across our dreams through
all our hopes of a good life. A chord in the dark air
in which we take our singing parts until bettered.

And on other hills, far away from there, could
that still be us, could it be anything as incredible
as us, persisting, setting a foot on the empty grave

of the music teacher who tunes his lute to the
chord of the wolves across the land asking
what is this Howl that we are left with what its resolution?

xii.

I remember… I forget what I remember.
Ah, Robyn, gentle Robyn, your soft locks
on my forehead and nobody said a word.

It's not a folksong. It's a technicality.
Six Canada geese in formation way above
Brighouse station, brilliant arrowhead finding its home.

On the riverside lawn where our parts agree
we sip Cuban cocktails served by black boys
in white jackets who know better than anyone

that you cannot force an ending on the bright air of ever
with nothing resolved into justice. For we are many
and will not forget. We are the them that doesn't.

xiii.

Press the cork back into the neck
and the day is concluded. Tomorrow,
Messiaen in Blackburn Cathedral and total crisis.

Total, inescapable, end, crisis. And why not?
Why after 300 years not? The gentle harmony
at the Labour Club confirms our sweet failure,

the crashing tones, the squeaking mice,
the unstoppable reproduction, *Gloria*
in excelsis and peace on earth, they all know

it's not happening. The dawn song
closes the festival as first light touches
the tips of the forest and the dancers go home.

The tired musicians case their viols knowing
that in the long night of their absence there
has been such violence. Twist the cork out and pour

another half glass no more, raise it to those who died
while we parodied. The gate in the long wall
is open, the nymphs are banging on the door,

the dead turn in their hotel beds knowing that for all
their work and hopes love lies cloven.
And not whosoever and not things happen

but specifically, by design, to create the enemies
needed as targets for the malice upon which all
their empire stands, and all their courts combine.

They have capped our hearts and closed our sight on
blinding detail, which gets us out of their way. We had best
march quietly on in thought, cap in hand.

There is a pavane that is the music of that march.
It rolls many times over. It presses against the lungs.
It speaks quietly to the nearest person, “Sandwiches and

beer when we get to Pontefract. We have not finished yet.”
“Thanks and joy to you. Nourish your patience, we have
some way to go yet.” “We shall never forgive them for this.”

xiv.

Goodbye, then, white dove. Goodbye clear, *luce*
serene clear *e chiare*, light, true speech, goodbye.
And yet the ground over yonder is rich with simplicity.

First sunlight cast along the canal represents
eight Canada geese as a golden flotilla.
Under their gold they worry and watch as usual.

What kills me in love is when
the world falls into the song and
laughs itself out again.

Sé que me muero, me muero de amor.
The gentle, best-meaning synapse lights its lamp.
And did those scarred and blistered feet.

xv.

I'll stop that now. I'll stop dying of love and,
so trimly dight with feathers like a lady bright
I'll sit alone, singing by night, in foreign tongue

Te whit, te whoo, te whit te whit te whoo. Are not
the final words of the *Agnus Dei* a desperate plea,
that we not be made to awaken from death?

We beg in the end this one favour,
save us from this savagery, to be roused
into a light not of this earth

and spoken to! what could be worse? To be
forced back into language. *Dona nobis pacem.*
Te whit, te whoo, te whit te whit te whoo.

Sweet Yorkshire owl, come join the chorus
and with the London wolves together we'll sing
a dirge for dying souls. Souls. Souls. Souls. Souls.

xvi.

Up to Old Chamber again by the shining road
bedecked in stone, gleaming in recent rain
and shaped exactly to the task. A product

of generations, like the vast underground
labyrinths created by the Cornish miners, like
a refugee support group at the very heart

of possible action within the bounds
of Greater Manchester. We pass the honesty box
where the old dog leaves us alone

and continue, the town down below,
Pinnacle Lane riding the shelving
of the upper valley – long and straight

between stone walls, and wet underfoot
at gated hollows. Open and empty road, no
ghosts in it now, no ancestors or authors.

They couldn't compete with the cold cruelty
of the carers, those whose duty it is
to care what becomes of us and couldn't less.

Unmeant words clog our ears, false promises
gag our throats. All we have learned
is being sent to waste and the road through Hell

never reaches the border. Up here we count our progress
in centuries, in stone sinking through earth.
O powerful western fallen star! speak to us,

comfort us, serve us our lunch, show us
a right of way through to the light at the end
of the night and a reason to bother thinking.

Walking, we go at walking speed, and so miss
nothing, the faint squeaking in the grass, the clicking
of gorse, the burning oilfield beyond the horizon.

Powerful western fallen star, lie down there,
on the town, flex your body to the angles
of hill and river, and listen. This town for

all its jubilee partakes of the condition of the nation.
Geese fly over, frogs crouch under, owls laugh in despair
at the heaven-bound tricksters that we failed to oppose

being too busy proving how radical we were.
Cast it aside and ride the upper lip
of an elegant clough all the way down to the Co-op.

So the walking ends and we turn in at our doors
and switch on the light and there are all the books in rows
trying to tell us what we could have done.

That night that band at that club. Seeking
signs of optimism. It was announced that
someone had just *had a baby*

and the place went mad. It seemed that
shining angels rose from between the floorboards
in bright uniforms, prepared to act.

And later the clicking of a passing train
along the valley. The skills people have.
The patience they endure.

Nine Poems

i.

It was the days of Sandy Denny,
who entered my sleep in the middle of the night
singing one star awake, that soon will fall
and in my darkness lit a candle and placed it
on the bedside table in a saucer of water.
And oh the toxic powder, the sexual fears,
the frozen streets, the hand that comes in
sideways and takes all, the food banks,
the lost grandchildren weeping on the moors,
the abandoned hope, the stuck to the pavement,
the can't afford the fare, the can't hear what you say,
the burning tower, the smashed saucer.

ii.

It was the days of Edgard Varèse.
I dreamt a whole war, and woke
to an empty street in first light,
and in Arabic, a beautiful language,
spoke my way past the new care homes
and agencies towards the open land.
The war was between artillery and artillery.
The worst thing was the quietness, with
a ticking noise and drum-taps between
enormous crashes full of brass bands
and exploding factories. The open lands
responded in Arabic, where have all the birds gone?

iii.

Those were the days of pale moon rising
over the apartment block opposite,
stormy weather on its way, stay
here with me. And all the choirs in the land
howled again in perfect accord
and all the bones buried in the land
"so close that one would touch another"
were entirely in our keeping. As the moon
mooned outside we conceived a future.
Letters and breves on finger pads
touching your cheek. Regarding your impudence.
It was different after we threw ourselves away.

iv.

We looked everywhere in the grass. It was the days
of Tony Hancock and we should be here somewhere.
Words stuck in glottis, only half pretending to be real,
we contradicted and steered hope into a wall shouting
Hey! who did that? You, everyone. I was there
and saw you, turning your self on the spit, a good meal
for any hungry aristocrat who never says
a word and doesn't pretend for a second to care
if we live (or what on) or die piecemeal.
So hoist the mainsail and stutter the chronicle of days
and swell those organs with radical pride and declare
we're going back to the home no longer there.

v.

Slowly through the stonewrack of Nab Hill,
and not a bird heard, not a shriek or a cheep
in all the abandoned quarries, where someone
thought of picking up the waste and building
wind-shelters where few ever go.
This hard, wet, cold, nothing land of
mud slopes and terrible grass, not asking
what we want. This aristocratic bogland
that lays its eggs and runs away, whose stones
make our tombs, ring cairns, sentences, dances,
memory dances on the marble floor all night
in the days of The Fitzwilliam Virginal Book.

vi.

Now the worm sleeps in its earth and the bat
rides the dark air and windows on the surface
of the canal speak of a warm wind from west.
And maybe a red flower on the windowsill
and maybe dignity and continuity. Soon
the last star will fade and dignity and honour
will be words we used to use. We use words
we can trust, that speak to a world that is,
and won't serve as artillery. The waves mock us
and the desert hisses, the hard moor grass
stands aside while slow cows file towards home.
These are the days of Les Filles de Illighadad.

vii.

Sweet slow cattle tread the mud towards home
where the mind is calm as the day fades
and the sheep sing chorales in the dark fields
and public truth still works. Don't tell them.
Don't move, don't tell anyone where the answer is,
one breath of it and we are listed, the black masque
advances up the fields smothering thought in noise
and will pursue us hooting to the ends of the earth.
And they shall have us, they shall finish us off
until we never were, we shall be smears of calcium
in lumps of clay under ring cairns, burning bright enough
to remind them after centuries that they lost the earth.

viii.

Sleep, little centipedes, while the earth rots,
dream of Manchester. Never since Angel Meadow
has there been such governmental slaughter,
the bodies scattered across the squares and
bundled in shop doorways through the winter
hope lost from the faces turning upwards
an underclass without ceremonies or recompense
and Palestinians forced out of their land to be
treated as vermin in Rochdale, and played with
by civil servants. Feed them a bit of hope and
snatch it back, Jack; who are not unkind people
by nature but deprived of mind space. Wake up.

ix.

Wake up everything you can think of.
Language for instance. Any language.
Swedish. Du som har mitt hela hjärte.
Work it out, until it smiles on you
and breaks your heart. Elolinola, that
fleeting smile, what became of your days?
I kept the images at bay for as long
as possible but here they come:
the black river crashing under the station
the burning huts on the horizon, the snowdrops
dead on time. The last of the wine, another century
of massacres, the hope extant in one blind rhyme.

Notes

Pennine Tales

Branwell Brontë was employed as "clerk in charge" of Luddendenfoot station in April 1842 and dismissed in 1843. The station was closed in 1962.

Wolf child. Not a young werewolf, but one of the many orphans left homeless after 1945 in the eastern European war zones and, gone feral, left to wander through the countryside, heading westwards in the hope of being taken in somewhere.

Hushings

Hushings are places where limestone has been exposed and broken for extraction of ore, or for burning into lime, by unleashing a rush of water down a hillside from a reservoir on higher ground. It produces a landscape of small conical hills.

Solveig's song. From Ibsen's *Peer Gynt*, music by Grieg. The words say, "I shall wait for you for ever. Though the seasons and the years come and go, still I shall wait for your return."

Dove sei, amato bene? "Where are you, much loved person?"

Ring Cairns

A ring cairn, or cairn circle, is a circular embankment built of stones, which encompasses an area used, originally or secondarily, for cremated burial deposits.

As with rosy steps the dawn advancing… Thomas Morell, in the libretto of Handel's *Theodora*.

Causied track. Causied short for causewayed. A footpath, in this case across a moor, paved with slabs of stone. They were made originally for workers to get from their homes on the high ground down to the mills in the valley.

Our long history on small scraps of paper: Lee Harwood.

Sé que me muero… I know that I am dying of love. Song by Lully from the "Ballet des Nations" attached to the end of Molière's *Le Bourgeois Gentilhomme* (not included in all modern editions).

"I'll stop this now…" This poem includes substantial content from the text of the madrigal "Sweet Suffolk owl…" by Thomas Vautor.

Powerful western fallen star: Whitman's form of address to Lincoln, when he died.

Nine Poems

Angel Meadow: see Part XII of my *Due North*, Shearsman Books 2015 (not included in *Collected Poems*).

Scribal Glosses
(homage to the Master of the Macclesfield Psalter)

(numerical references, e.g. 9/1:
page nine/line 1)

Pennine Tales

9/1 *flicker through the trees*
"...making a red punctuation in the cursive night..."

11/8 *my sisters*
... saluted me, and referred me to the coming on of time.

12/12 *the hymn of last or lasting hope*
= the song of delayed passengers (16/10)

13/2
Etymologically the words *complicit, accomplice* imply intent to harm (?).

14
The transition from *Wuthering Heights* via Ted Hughes to penguins was effected by the thought of Modern Poets, how they transform themselves from weeping into frozen walls.

15/5 *mournful calling falling sound*
"...calls far and long falling as I focus on the fact." But that was a curlew.

18/1 *shine into tomorrow*
Shine on, harvest moon.

19/3-4 *hands over the hilltop…*
or hands across the sea when both of us are stone.

19/8 *and thus sang the old man:*
Kiere wider, heil'ge Nacht! Holde Träume, kehret wider!

26/1 *all you little vermin*
Come all you rolling minstrels And together, we will try To rouse the spirit of the earth And move the rolling sky.

26/12 *the last waltz*
… or lasting quickstep

27/1 *pale primroses…*
… that die unmarried, ere they can behold Bright Phoebus in his strength

27/2 *with violets intermixed*
... but they withered all when my father died

27/12 *…where our numbers are called in finally*
Come in number 19 your time is up.

28/1 *There is a History in all men's lives…*
Henry IV 2, iii/1. Then let us meet them like necessities.

36/1-2 *A motet by Antoine Brumel:*
Salve Regina

37/7 *the swans singing goodbye on the reservoir*
Farewell all joys, O death come close my eyes.

38/2 *and one of them says to the other*
Where shall we our breakfast take?

39/9 *and bugle*
the trumpet shall sound, and we shall be changed

40/11 *the black grouse*
The grouse around here are red, but there was a problem with the phonetics. They kept shouting GOBACK! (to where you once belonged).

44/4 *And all the voices make one mutual cry*
I never heard So musical a discord, such sweet thunder.

44/7 *At Swinside...*
SD17168817

45/1 *You tourists who come and go*
Is it nothing to you, all ye that pass by?

51/10 *the last kind thought* (by Geeshie Wiley).
It is here assumed that the "Windrush" deportations, since they could have no effect on the relevant statistics, were undertaken purely as a display, of the capacity for brutality, in case we needed reminding.

52/2
Only remembered: for what we have done
Shallow Brown: You're going to leave me

55/1 *report anything suspicious*
Keeping the anxiety level pumped up.

55/14 *the world's thought-task*
… this great and wide sea, wherein are things creeping innumerable, both small and great beasts.

55/14 *the world's thought-task*
A great ship setting out for the far side of the ocean. Ship is eyes.

57/18 *bobbing up and down*
aka *Sons of the Sea.*

63/13 *look down low*
Where nobody can find me. Where nobody can hurt me.

66/7 *the riverside lawn*
This must be at the back of Trinity College, Cambridge, when they lit the lanterns and sang from the flotilla, *Draw on sweet Night, best friend unto those cares That do arise from painfull melancholy.*

67/10-11 *The dawn song closes the festival*
And I'll be a star in the sky, shining faintly above the forest

69/12 *And did those scarred and blistered feet*
Did they what? Did they march to Versailles? And seven times round the walls? And did they blow their horns and shout?

71/3 *shaped exactly to the task*
A dip each side for the cart wheels and a hump in the middle for the horse.

71/4-5 *like the vast underground labyrinths created by the Cornish miners*
See covers of both volumes of *Collected Poems* (2018).

77 *Sandy Denny*
And then she turned homeward with one star awake, As the swan in the evening moves over the black reservoir and out of sight.

78 *Edgard Varèse*
Un grand sommeil noir. And see Cocteau, *Discourse du Grand Sommeil* (1916-1918) and Wyndham Lewis in *Rude Assignment* (1950): "The war was a sleep, deep and animal, in which I was visited by images of an order new to me."

81/5
The wind-shelters are also punctuation marks.

82 *Les Filles de Illighadad*
https://www.youtube.com/watch?v=Ff4jRjbuCm8

85
the black river under the station les côtes de la misère
the snowdrops the borders of time
the last of the wine the last of Nora Batty
hope extant changed, into something near and far
blind rhyme Now, now that the sun hath veil'd his light And bid the world good night

The glossing process can continue indefinitely, and at a certain point will be taken out of my hands.

Acknowledgements

Both *Pennine Tales* and *Hushings* were first published, in earlier versions, as pamphlets by Calder Valley Poetry (Bob Horne) in 2016 and 2017, forming a gratifying welcome to West Yorkshire. Poems and sections from *Ring Cairns* were published in Poetry Salzburg Review, PN Review and Free Verse. *Nine Poems* appeared on the website Blackbox Manifold (Adam Piette). I'm grateful to the editors and staff of these publications.